Helen Battelley

50

Series editor
ALISTAIR
BRYCE-CLEGG

fantastic ideas for
songs and rhymes

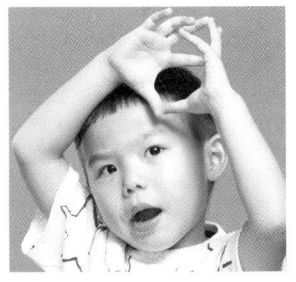

FEATHERSTONE

FEATHERSTONE
Bloomsbury Publishing Plc
50 Bedford Square, London, WC1B 3DP, UK
29 Earlsfort Terrace, Dublin 2, Ireland

BLOOMSBURY, FEATHERSTONE and the Feather logo are trademarks of Bloomsbury Publishing Plc

First published in Great Britain, 2021 by Bloomsbury Publishing Plc

A catalogue record for this book is available from the British Library

ISBN: PB: 978-1-4729-7685-7; ePDF: 978-1-4729-7684-0

2 4 6 8 10 9 7 5 3 1

Designed by Lynda Murray
Printed and bound in India by Replika Press Pvt. Ltd.

To find out more about our authors and books visit www.bloomsbury.com and sign up for
our newsletters

Contents

Introduction

Parents, carers and educators introduce young children to rhymes and action songs as part of an ongoing tradition passed from generation to generation. I recall with fondness the songs I sang as a young girl, firstly with my parents and carers and then with my peers. My first childhood memory is being swung upside down to a rhyme about fishing in the deep blue sea!

As a parent, I passed those rhymes and action songs onto my children, who showed a preference for the most active and thrill-enhancing ones! Then, as a music and movement specialist these songs became part of my practice, and through academic study I understood the value and impact of such activities.

Frequently we observe children singing interactive rhymes in playgrounds. Many actions songs are universal, shared across cultures and symbolic of early childhood. When travelling and working abroad I have witnessed first-hand the pleasure and enjoyment all children gain from participating in such activities, with onlooking children gravitating towards other children, wanting to share in the experience.

This book aims to provide you with an insight into the benefits of singing rhymes and action songs. It includes 50 songs and rhymes to get you started, combining some everyday favourites with some of my own versions you may not have heard of!

The benefits of music and movement

Action songs and rhymes are the primary origin of musical entrainment, which is the ability to synchronise our actions and movements to music and rhythm. Research demonstrates that singing and playing music together provides children with a sense of inclusivity: a feeling that they are part of a group and that they belong. Studies have shown that babies and infants have the ability to feel rhythm in their bodies, presenting a physiological response to music. We also know that music is a powerful tool for motivating and empowering children. Also, listening to music and rhythms we enjoy releases dopamine, the reward inducing hormone.

In early childhood, learning generally takes place in social settings. Whether this is in an early years setting or a family home, young children will spend most of their waking hours in the company of others. The ability to share space and time with others is essential in human development, as we are a sociable species! Many of the songs and rhymes in this book help to foster a sense of social engagement and cohesion.

Also, introducing children to singing from an early age promotes the development of early language skills. Studies have shown that music instruction accelerates brain development in early childhood, in the areas responsible for sound and speech perception, reading, and language development.

However, vocabulary and language development are not the only developmental areas supported through rhymes and action songs. For example, the rhymes in this book also:

* introduce children to mathematical concepts, such as number ordering, patterns and sequencing

* develop children's knowledge of the world around them

* provide opportunities for physical activity and self-care.

Most importantly, music facilitates communication beyond words: it is the language we all speak!

The adult role

Early childhood movement and dance is often mirrored behaviour, modelled on peer observation, where children copy the actions they see. Therefore, your contribution as a facilitator cannot be overstated.

Providing young children with a range of movement experiences within a secure, nurturing environment is the best start in life for every child. Embedding music, rhythm, physical activity and movement into your daily routines (rather than as standalone sessions) will promote learning in all early childhood developmental domains. Create time and space for children to explore their creativity and musical expression.

Finally, don't worry if you don't know or remember the tune of a rhyme. The children in your care are your biggest fans, regardless of whether you are pitch perfect or not! Don't be afraid to be creative and make up your own tunes. You could also do a quick online search for the songs in this book, which will provide a wide range of different versions. When you sing, keep the tempo slow to start with then increase it once the children become more familiar with the song or rhyme.

How to use this book

Before you start any activity, read through everything on the page so you are familiar with the whole activity and what you might need to plan in advance. The pages are all organised in the same way.

What you need lists the resources required for the activity. You should also ensure the space you're using is always clean and hazard-free. If possible, ensure children have plenty of space to move. You can also explore opportunities to make the rhymes 'bigger' and more physical, rather than sitting down with hand actions and gestures.

What to do provides step-by-step instructions.

Health & Safety: In many cases there are no specific hazards involved in completing the activity, and your usual health and safety measures should be enough. In others there are particular issues to be noted and addressed.

What's in it for the children? lists some of the benefits children will gain from the activities and how these will contribute to their learning.

Taking it forward gives ideas for additional activities on the same theme, or for developing the activity further. These will be particularly useful for things that have gone especially well or where children show a real interest. In many cases they use the same resources, and in every case they have been designed to extend learning and broaden the children's experiences.

Top tips give a brief word of advice or helpful tip that could make all the difference to the experience of the activity for you and the children.

1, 2, 3, 4, 5
Moving individual fingers

What you need:

- A drum (optional)

What's in it for the children?

Combining both single digit movements (counting fingers) and coordinated hand movements (opening and closing arms) will boost children's vestibular system. Our vestibular system (located in the inner ear) is our inbuilt spirit level. It enables us to move, play, learn, rest and explore: essential aspects of early childhood development.

Taking it forward

- As the children become more familiar with the song, offer pauses to encourage them to finish the lines.

- Use a drum or clap the numbers, ensuring the children have time to count each number.

- Try making a fish pond. Draw, colour and cut out some large fish, then attach a paperclip to the end, near the mouth. Attach a piece of string to a stick with a small magnet tied to the end. Do not leave children unsupervised with these. Then invite the children to see how many fish they can catch.

What to do:

1. With the children sitting on the floor or standing, sing the song together using the actions as detailed below. Sing the song slowly, to allow time for the children to grasp the fine motor skills required for the actions.

One, two, three, four, five,
(Hold fingers up as you count them)
Once I caught a fish alive,
(Place your hands together and swish them like a fish)
Six, seven, eight, nine, ten,
(Count the fingers on your other hand)
Then I let it go again.
(Open your hands to let the fish go)

Why did you let it go?
(Display your hands out to the side)
Because it bit my fingers so.
(Put your hands on your hips)
Which finger did it bite?
(Display your hands out to the side)
This little finger on my right.
(Raise your little finger on your right hand)

1, 2, 3, 4, 5... Shark!

Adding a new verse to a traditional song

What you need:

- A drum (optional)
- Puppets (optional)

Top tip

To reduce the time spent sitting, sing this song standing in a circle and exaggerate the actions even more.

What's in it for the children?

This new ending to a traditional rhyme adds surprise and excitement and provides the children with the confidence to create their own rhymes. They often love to include an element of mild peril!

Taking it forward

- You may wish to use puppets alongside the rhyme.

- Offer the children the choice to create their own version: can they think of a different scary creature? For example, 'Once I caught a lion alive.'

- Play the fishing game as outlined on page 6. This time, add four paperclips to a cut-out shark and place it in the 'pond' with the fish. The children should try not to fish out the shark!

What to do:

1. Continue the song from page 6, with an additional verse!

2. This time, add a physical development opportunity and invite the children to step as they count the numbers.

3. Use the same actions as described on page 6, but this time pretend to be a shark by putting your hands together on top of your head with your hands pointing up to imitate a dorsal fin.

4. Wag your finger and look alarmed when you sing 'I won't be doing that again!'.

One, two, three, four, five,
Once I caught a shark alive,
Six, seven, eight, nine, ten,
I won't be doing that again!

Five Little Ducks

Practising counting and sequencing

What you need:

- Hand puppets, stickers on fingers, or toy ducks (optional)

Top tip ⭐

Research has shown that children who use their fingers for counting perform better in later mathematical learning.

What to do:

1. Prior to singing the song, hold up five fingers on one hand and count them with the children. If you have props, count them too.

2. Sing the song with the actions. If you are using duck props, remove one duck as you sing each verse.

   Five little ducks went swimming one day,
   (Show five fingers)
   Over the hills and far away,
   (Move your arm up and down)
   Mummy duck said 'Quack, quack, quack, quack!'
   (Gesture quacking with your fingers and thumb)
   And four little ducks came swimming back.

3. Repeat the song, removing a duck or finger each time. You can also change 'mummy duck' to 'daddy duck' or 'nanny duck', etc.

4. When you get to 'no little ducks went swimming one day…' you could sing very loudly 'And five little ducks came swimming back' for a happy ending!

What's in it for the children?

This is an excellent song for emotional development and attachment. It also supports counting and number ordering. Children will learn to isolate fingers, requiring coordination and control.

Taking it forward

- For older children, chose five children to demonstrate being the ducks (an adult can be the mummy or daddy duck). Each verse one duck 'swims' off to another area of the room.

- You could use the theme of the song to introduce conversations around safety with older children, highlighting 'stranger danger'.

- Include a 'hook a duck' activity alongside the song.

Chick Chick Chicken

Wiggling and flapping like a chicken

What you need:

- Egg shakers (optional)

What's in it for the children?

Role play promotes active expression. The actions also support muscle development, coordination and control. Squatting is great for stretching and opening up the spine.

Taking it forward

- Using egg shakers is a great way to enhance the song.

- At the end of the song, hide the egg shaker underneath you and exclaim, 'Ta-da! We've laid an egg!'

- Introduce a vegan alternative!

  Chick, chick, chick, chick, chickpea,

  Make a little hummus for me.

  Chick, chick, chick, chick, chickpea,

  I want some for my tea,

  I haven't had any breakfast,

  Nothing since half past three,

  So chick, chick, chick, chick, chickpea,

  Make a little hummus for me!

What to do:

1. With the children sitting or squatting, demonstrate the actions to the song.

   Chick, chick, chick, chick, chicken,
   (Bend and flap your arms)
   Lay a little egg for me.
   (Wiggle as if laying an egg)
   Chick, chick, chick, chick, chicken,
   I want one for my tea.
   (Point to yourself)
   I haven't had an egg since breakfast,
   (Fold your arms)
   And now it's half past three.
   (Point to a clock/watch)
   So chick, chick, chick, chick, chicken,
   Lay a little egg for me.

2. Once the children have mastered the actions, try doing it standing up.

3. Encourage the children to extend the actions by walking around, wiggling and stamping their feet.

Old MacDonald

Introducing sign language

What you need:

- Small world animals, soft toys or puppets (optional)

What to do:

1. For younger children, sing the song and introduce the animal sounds and actions.

2. For older children, use body percussion for the rhythm, gently slapping alternate thighs.

   Old MacDonald had a farm, E-I-E-I-O!
   And on that farm he had a dog, E-I-E-I-O!
   With a woof, woof here and a woof, woof there,
   Here a woof, there a woof,
   Everywhere a woof-woof,
   Old MacDonald had a farm, E-I-E-I-O!

3. Use the British Sign Language (BSL) actions as you continue the song and sign the words for different animals. You could use small world animals to help you demonstrate.

   Dog: point both index and middle fingers down.

   Cat: use your fingers to stroke whiskers outwards.

   Sheep: draw little circles with your little fingers next to your temples.

   Cow: stick up your little fingers and thumbs to imitate horns.

   Duck: make a beak with one hand.

   Pig: make a fist and circle it near your nose.

What's in it for the children?

This song builds children's knowledge and understanding of the world as they learn about farm life and match the animals with their sounds. Creating the animal sounds will help develop children's oracy and early language skills.

Taking it forward

- Pause when you sing, 'He had a…' and invite the children to suggest an animal and offer a sound.

- 'Walk the song', follow-the-leader style, with the children in a line, each holding the next person's waist. Pause at 'He had a…' and invite the child at the front of the line to choose an animal. Everyone makes the animal's sound, then the child at the front moves to the back and the song continues.

Two Little Dicky Birds

Wiggling fingers

What you need:

- No additional resources needed for this activity

What's in it for the children?

The children develop increased dexterity, control and coordination, putting to use all the muscles in their hands. This can boost fine motor skills, needed for early writing skills. The song also helps children to understand object permanence (when you can't see things, does that mean they have disappeared?).

Taking it forward

- There is a trick to enhance this rhyme which promotes children's curiosity. Add a little sticker onto each index finger (ideally draw a little bird face onto the sticker). When the birds 'fly away', demonstrate to the children how to hold onto their index finger within their closed hand and release their middle finger, creating an illusion that the birds have flown away. Once they have mastered the skill, they can trick others with their magic!
- Look online for some simple magic tricks to teach the children.

What to do:

1. Start by holding your hands out in front of you and wiggling your index fingers to show 'Peter and Paul'.

2. Sing the song together, inviting the children to use their fingers for the actions.

   Two little dickie birds sitting on a wall,
   (Show both index fingers)
   One named Peter, one named Paul,
   (Wiggle each one in turn)
   Fly away Peter! Fly away Paul!
   (Fly each finger away, behind your back)
   Come back Peter! Come back Paul!
   (Bring each finger back)

3. Change the animals to frogs:

   Two little frogs sitting on a log,
   One named Zig and one named Zog,
   Hop away Zig! Hop away Zog!
   Come back Zig! Come back Zog!

Hickory Dickory Dock

Making tick-tock movements

What you need:

- A metronome (optional)
- A mouse finger puppet (optional)

Top tip

Sing this song outside and draw a clock face on the floor using chalk. Children can sing the song standing on the numbers.

What's in it for the children?

This song has a strong recurrent beat and will allow children to imitate the rhythm. The actions promote musical entrainment (this is when people synchronise their movements to music).

Taking it forward

- Using a mouse puppet increases the children's imagination and involvement.
- As the children become more familiar with the song, leave pauses to allow them to finish the lines.
- Play a game of cat and mouse using a parachute. One child, the mouse, hides under the parachute while another child, the cat, tries to catch them. The rest of the children shake the parachute to make it more difficult!

What to do:

1. If you have a metronome, use the beat to assist with the rhythm of the song.

2. The actions to this song increase in complexity with each verse. For the first verse, use one straight arm stretched up for the clock, with the other hand as the mouse running up and down. 'Tick tock' your arms at the end.

   Hickory dickory dock,
   The mouse ran up the clock.
   The clock struck one,
   The mouse ran down,
   Hickory dickory dock, tick tock, tick tock, tick tock.

3. For the second verse, drop your arm quickly to show the branch snapping. For 'tick, tee', wiggle the top half of your body.

   Hickory dickory dee,
   The mouse ran up the tree.
   The branch: it snapped,
   The mouse was trapped,
   Hickory dickory dee, tick tee, tick tee, tick tee.

4. For the third verse, walk your fingers up your legs. Imitate eating cheese and having wobbly knees, then walk your fingers back down your legs.

   Hickory dickory dare,
   The mouse ran up the chair.
   He ate some cheese,
   Had wobbly knees,
   Hickory dickory dare, tick tare,
   tick tare, tick tare.

Baa Baa Black Sheep

Counting with fingers

What you need:

- Puppets (optional)

Top tip

When singing the rhyme with children, occasionally omit the end of the line and invite the children to finish it. This supports memory development and language skills.

What's in it for the children?

Demonstrating counting on fingers is an important learning mechanism; it transforms abstract mathematical concepts into tangible learning. Studies have shown that counting and finger games can help improve children's mathematical performance.

Taking it forward

- Act out the story, for example using puppets, bringing an element of role play.
- Develop children's curiosity about how things are made and in different fabrics and textures. Ask, 'Where does this come from?' Invite them to look at the labels in their clothes to find out where they were made and from which fabric.

What to do:

1. Sing this song to the tune of 'Twinkle Twinkle Little Star'. Many similar versions are sung around the world.

2. Nod your head for 'Yes sir' and use three fingers to show three bags, then one finger for each character.

   Baa baa black sheep,
   Have you any wool?
   Yes sir, yes sir,
   Three bags full.
   One for the master,
   And one for the dame,
   And one for the little boy
   Who lives down the lane.

3. Introduce a variation:

   Baa baa black sheep,
   Have you any wool?
   Yes, sir, yes, sir,
   Three bags full.
   One for a jumper,
   And one for a frock
   And one for the little boy
   With a hole in his sock.

Peter Rabbit

Thinking about facial expressions

What you need:

- A toy rabbit or finger puppet (optional)

What's in it for the children?

The song involves children thinking about facial features and uses complex hand movements, developing fine motor control. The song provides opportunities for movement across the midline axis, which boosts development on both sides of the brain. The story of the song has a comedic value for children and shared humour can help develop their social skills.

Taking it forward

- Invite the children to create their own movements for the song. Encourage them to stand up and demonstrate their actions to others.

- Using sticky tape and cotton wool, invite the children to make bunny tails which they can stick to their bottoms!

What to do:

1. Invite the children to sit down and demonstrate the actions.

2. Try the actions as detailed below: if you don't have props, you can use hand gestures to support the rhyme.

   Peter Rabbit has a fly upon his nose, (x3)

   (Put your hands on your head as rabbit ears; use a finger as a fly and point to your nose)

   So he flipped it and he flapped it and the fly flew away.

   (Use alternate hands to imitate flapping it away)

   Floppy ears and curly whiskers, (x3)

   (Put your hands on your head, then twirl your fingers)

   He flipped it and he flapped it and the fly flew away.

   (Use your finger to imitate the fly flying away)

I Had a Little Turtle

Having fun with bubbles

What you need:

- Bubbles (optional). For example, add soap suds in a bowl of water and whisk

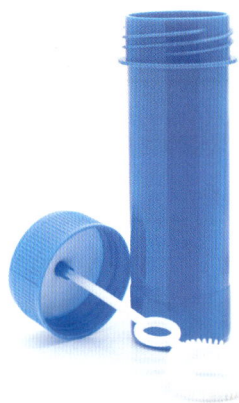

What's in it for the children?

The actions help the children understand the words of the song, strengthening language development and aiding their memory of the lyrics. If you are using bubbles, these are good for developing children's hand-eye coordination and for strengthening the muscles around the eyes, as children track the bubbles.

Taking it forward

- If you are using soap suds and a whisk, encourage the children to use the whisk in a bowl of soapy water for 'bubble, bubble'. The harder they whisk, the higher the bubbles will go!

- Use a bubble machine or bubble liquid and invite the children to pop the bubbles.

What to do:

1. Introduce the song to the children sitting on the floor, then move to standing.

2. Follow the actions as shown below.

   I had a little turtle,
   (Make a turtle with one hand flat and the other hand in a fist on top)
   His name was Tiny Tim.
   I put him in the bathtub,
   (Imitate lowering Tiny Tim into the bath)
   To see if he could swim.
   (Pretend to swim)

   He drank up all the water,
   (Pretend to drink)
   And ate a bar of soap.
   (Take a large gulp)
   And now he's in his bed,
   (Place your hands to side of your head)
   With bubbles in his throat.
   (Gently hold your throat)
   Bubble, bubble, bubble... (x3)
   ... Pop!
   (Clap loudly)

Crabs and Starfish

Imagining being underwater

What you need:

- Blue ribbons (optional)

Top tip

You could play some 'under the sea' music for the children to dance to and give them blue ribbons to make waves.

What's in it for the children?

This is such a fun song, which uses a wealth of arm and hand movements to develop upper body strength, coordination and control. Learning about different sea creatures will develop children's curiosity about the natural world.

Taking it forward

- Invite the children to create their own movements for each creature.

- Progress to full body movements, singing the song very slowly to allow enough time for them to establish the movements. Here are some ideas:
  - **Crabs:** Walk on all fours, bellies facing up.
  - **Starfish:** Lay flat on the floor.
  - **Shark:** Glide around the room, 'snapping' your arms shut.
  - **Octopus:** Wiggle your arms and legs.
  - **Penguins.** Waddle with straight arms and legs.
  - **Dolphins:** Imitate diving with your palms together.

What to do:

1. Sing the song slowly at first until the children are familiar with all the actions. The song can be sung to the tune of 'Frère Jacques'.

   Crabs and starfish, (x2)
   Big shark too, (x2)
   Octopus and penguins, (x2)
   Dolphins too. (x2)

2. Start with the children sitting and using hand actions and progress to standing up using whole body actions. You may wish to practise the actions for each animal before singing the song.

   - **Crab:** Snap your fingers and thumbs together like claws.
   - **Starfish:** Spread out your arms and legs.
   - **Shark:** Snap your outstretched arms together.
   - **Octopus:** Wiggle your arms.
   - **Penguins:** Hold your arms by your sides and shake them.
   - **Dolphins:** Pretend to dive with your palms together.

Down by the River

Enjoying a boogie!

What you need:

- A tambourine
- Shakers or maracas

Top tip

This song is a variation of the popular rhyme 'Down in the Jungle'. You could sing both variations.

What's in it for the children?

This song provides children with a wealth of vocabulary content to boost language skills. This song has a fun upbeat rhythm and children will find it hard to sit still to the 'boogie woogie'!

Taking it forward

- Repeat the song standing up to encourage dancing to the rhythm of the song.
- Provide a child with a whistle for the 'squeak' sounds – this provides lots of fun!
- Invite the children to create some actions or a dance to the song.

What to do:

1. Sit the children in a circle and invite them to choose an instrument.

2. The adult introduces the song using a tambourine to show the movements (a tambourine is louder than the shakers, so this will help to reinforce the rhythm). Start with a slow tempo.

3. Ask the children to do three slow shakes for the 'squeak, squeak, squeak' and then a continuous shake for 'boogie woogie'.

   Down by the river where nobody goes,
   There were three little field mice washing their clothes,
   With a rub-a-dub here and a rub-a-dub there,
   That's the way the field mice wash their clothes.
   With a squeak, squeak, squeak, boogie woogie, (x3)
   That's the way the field mice wash their clothes.

4. Repeat the song with 'two little field mice', then 'one little field mouse', decreasing the volume of the singing and shaking each time.

The Farmer's in His Den

Singing while moving in a circle

What you need:

- **Space to stretch and move**

What's in it for the children?

This song provides a rich environment for children to build relationships with others. Moving together in a circle improves their spatial skills and awareness of others around them, as they learn to coordinate their bodies to move sideways and sing simultaneously. Holding hands also supports emotional development.

Taking it forward

- Introduce props to encourage role play.
- Invite the children to think of other animals on a farm and the associated sounds.
- Invite the children to walk clockwise and anticlockwise in the circle.
- Play 'Squeak piggy, squeak!'. Ask the children to cover their eyes and select one child to hide behind a wall or door with an adult. Once the chosen child is out of sight, the others can open their eyes and call 'Squeak piggy, squeak!' The hidden child squeaks and the rest of the group must try and identify the child from their squeaks.

What to do:

1. Select a child to be the farmer.

2. Invite the other children to hold hands and make a large circle with the farmer in the middle.

3. Sing the song and walk slowly around together in a circle.

   The farmer's in his den,
   The farmer's in his den,
   E-AH-A-DE-OH,
   The farmer's in his den.

4. Repeat with variations, allowing the farmer to choose a child to join them in the middle of the circle each time.

   - *The farmer wants a friend…*
   - *The friend wants a child…*
   - *The child wants a dog…*
   - *The dog wants a bone…*
   - *We all clap the bone…*

5. Encourage everyone to clap when you sing 'We all clap the bone' and repeat the song until everyone who wants a turn has had a turn.

Open Them, Shut Them

Practising hand movements

What you need:

- No additional resources needed for this activity

What to do:

1. Follow the directions of the song. Keep it slow at first until the children become familiar with the song.

2. For 'open' and 'shut', flash your hands open and then scrunch them closed.

3. For 'creep', walk your fingers up your body to your chin.

4. At the end of the song, cover your mouth with your hands.

   Open them, shut them, (x2)
   Give a little clap, clap, clap.
   Shut them, open them, (x2)
   Lay them in your lap, lap, lap.
   Creep them, creep them, (x2)
   Up to your little chin, chin, chin.
   Open up your little mouth…
   But… Do not put them in!

What's in it for the children?

This action song offers an introduction to positional language. The song encourages plentiful movement of the hand muscles, helping to develop fine motor skills. This song can also provide a chance to discuss hygiene and hand washing.

Taking it forward

- As the children become more familiar with this rhyme, they may start to do it independently.

Health & Safety

It's a good idea for children to wash their hands before and after this song.

If You're Happy and You Know it

Getting children active

What you need:

- Space to stretch and move

Top tip

Invite the children to create their own happy song with their own actions, e.g. 'if you're happy and you know it spin around'.

What's in it for the children?

The repeated actions will support the development of the vestibular system (see page 6 for more information). This song is great fun and helps children to be physically active and practise body percussion.

Taking it forward

- Invite the children to create new movements, such as turning around or jumping up and down.

- To develop social interaction and encourage turn-taking, ask children to face partners and clap together in a 'high ten' during the song.

- Invite a discussion on the topic of 'What makes you happy?'. You may like to explore other emotions too.

What to do:

1. Stand up and introduce the song by singing it slowly and demonstrating the actions: clapping, stamping, nodding and finally shouting 'We are!'.

2. Sing the song together, encouraging the children to copy your movements until they become familiar with the song.

   If you're happy and you know it clap your hands, (x2)

   If you're happy and you know it and you really want to show it,

   If you're happy and you know it clap your hands.

   If you're happy and you know it stamp your feet...

   If you're happy and you know it nod your head...

   If you're happy and you know it shout 'We are!'...

   If you're happy and you know it do all four...

Wind the Bobbin Up

Moving in different directions

What you need:

- No additional resources needed for this activity

Top tip ⭐

Explain to the children what a bobbin is and what it does. To demonstrate, encourage them to wind wool around a tube. This also develops their hand muscles.

What's in it for the children?

Children can discover new ways of moving and responding to rhythm. Movements with changing directions require coordination and control, which are fundamental for early writing skills. Counting and clapping will help them think about quantity and number ordering.

Taking it forward

- Partner the children and ask them to sit facing each other to practise mirroring each other.

- Boost some children's confidence by selecting a few children to sing the song to others.

- Begin singing sitting down and then progress to standing, encouraging bigger movements.

What to do:

1. Ensure each child has plenty of space.

2. Sing the song slowly at first to demonstrate the actions. Encourage children to roll their hands in one direction for 'Wind the bobbin up' and then the other direction for 'Wind it back again'.

3. The children can pull their hands out to the side and clap three times in time to the song.

4. Invite them to point to the ceiling, floor, window and door as you sing the song together.

Wind the bobbin up, (x2)
Pull, pull, clap, clap, clap.
Wind it back again, (x2)
Pull, pull, clap, clap, clap.
Point to the ceiling,
Point to the floor,
Point to the window,
Point to the door.
Clap your hands together: one, two, three.
Lay your hands upon your knees.

Roly Poly
Rolling hands and balls

What you need:

- Squidgy balls (optional)

Top tip

Try this activity with light-up balls and turn out the lights. This is great sensory fun.

What's in it for the children?

This is an ideal song for developing children's shoulder and arm muscles and postural control. The change in tempo will assist them with musical understanding and rhythm: this also supports language development. The positional language provides children with an opportunity to develop early mathematical concepts.

Taking it forward

- Introduce 'squidgy balls' and encourage the children to roll the ball as below:

  - *Roly poly up* (Roll the ball up your body.)
  - *Roly poly down* (Roll the ball down your body.)
  - *Roly poly in* (Roll the ball on the floor towards you.)
  - *Roly poly out* (Roll the ball away.)
  - *Roly poly ever so slowly* (Roll the ball slowly on your tummy or on the floor.)
  - *Roly poly ever so quickly* (Roll the ball quickly on your tummy or on the floor.)

What to do:

1. With the children sitting on the floor, demonstrate the actions as you sing the song.

   Roly poly up,
   (Roll your hands around, moving them up)
   Roly poly down,
   (Roll your hands down)
   Roly poly in,
   (Bring your hands towards your body)
   Roly poly out
   (Push your hands away from your body)
   Roly poly, ever so slowly,
   (Roll your hands slowly)
   Roly poly, ever so quickly.
   (Roll your hands quickly)

The Shaky Song

Shaking instruments and bodies

What you need:

- **Hand-held shakers**

What's in it for the children?

Responding to rhythm will develop children's musicality and playing music as a group builds their social skills. The song also covers a wealth of positional and directional language, which is helpful for learning early mathematical concepts. Listening and understanding skills are also practised as they listen and respond to directions.

Taking it forward

- Remove the instruments and ask the children to shake their bodies and make sounds using body percussion.

- Try replacing shaking with jumping, hopping, crawling, twirling, creeping, dancing, clapping, rubbing, shrugging, wiggling, rolling, and so on.

What to do:

1. With the children seated on the floor, provide each child with a shaker, ideally one shaker for each hand.

2. Encourage the children to shake to the rhythm of the song and stop every time you say 'stop'. Leave a long pause after 'stop' before singing the final line.

   Let's shake and shake and shake and stop,
   Shake and shake and shake and stop,
   Shake and shake and shake and stop,
   Now let's shake some more.

3. Change the tempo and pitch of the song. For example, sing it quietly, loudly, quickly and slowly.

4. If children have a shaker in each hand, replace 'shake' with 'tap' and explore different tapping possibilities. For example, children could tap high, low, in front, behind, quietly, loudly, soft, hard, fast and slow, and so on.

Tommy Thumb

Isolating fingers and thumbs

What you need:

- Bubble wrap (optional)

What's in it for the children?

This song allows children to practise isolating their fingers, which strengthens their hand muscles and is useful preparation for writing. Singing the song together enhances social competence and confidence.

Taking it forward

- Try using bubble wrap! When you sing 'How do you do?' encourage the children to use different fingers to pop the bubbles.

- If you are using bubble wrap, try to find as many innovative ways as possible to pop the bubbles. For example, children could jump, use their elbows or bottoms, or crawl over the bubbles.

- Use finger painting to support the song. Children could dip different fingers in the paint and apply it to paper.

 Health & Safety

Always supervise children when using plastics or small parts. Never leave them unattended.

What to do:

1. Sit down with the children and introduce the song.

2. Start with hands behind your back and follow the movements as shown.

3. First use your thumb to sing the song.

   Tommy Thumb, (x2)
   (Look around with hands behind your back)
   Where are you?
   Here I am, (x2)
   (Reveal one thumb, then the other)
   How do you do?
   (Wiggle one thumb, then the other)

4. Continue the song, revealing the other fingers one by one, before showing them all together for the final verse.

   Peter Pointer...
   Toby Tall...
   Ruby Ring...
   Baby Small...
   Fingers all...

Two Little Eyes

Mapping body parts

What you need:

- A mirror (optional)

Top tip

Add a few drops of lavender essential oil onto a flannel or cloth next to you while you sing this song. This will stimulate the children's sense of smell and create a calm environment.

What to do:

1. Ask permission to touch a child's eyes, ears, nose and mouth, demonstrating on yourself first.

2. For younger children, lay a child on the floor on their back. Use your index finger to gently follow the directions of the rhyme as indicated.

3. Maintain eye contact with the child for the duration of the song.

4. You may wish to introduce a mirror and encourage children to identify their own facial features by using the actions below on their own faces.

Two little eyes to look around,
(Gently circle eyes with your forefingers)
Two little ears to hear each sound,
(Trace along the temple and behind the ears)
One little nose to smell what's sweet,
(Trace from the forehead to the tip of the nose)
And one little mouth which likes to eat.
(Draw around the mouth and gently tap the lips)

What's in it for the children?

This calming rhyme can be used to stimulate the facial muscles through massage, developing a secure attachment between adult and child. This song can also develop children's proprioceptive sense and their body mapping skills. Proprioception is our understanding of where we are in space. Body mapping is about our perception of where our body parts are, what they do and how they move.

Taking it forward

- Encourage older children to replicate the actions on teddies or dolls.

- Use the song to assist in mark making and body mapping by asking the children to draw their faces on paper.

- Try using feathers to gently touch the face.

✚ Health & Safety

Ensure your hands are clean and warm in preparation for this song.

Ten Fat Sausages

Thinking about maths

What you need:

- **No additional resources needed for this activity**

What's in it for the children?

This song is great for developing children's knowledge of subtraction, counting in twos, doubling and halving. Using fingers to count builds their mathematical understanding and provides a sturdy mechanism for future mathematical learning.

Taking it forward

- Divide the children into two groups. Provide one group with drums or claves (a percussion instrument consisting of two sticks) and invite the other group to sing the song. The percussion group must play the sounds for 'pop' and 'bang' at the right moment, developing their listening skills. Swap groups afterwards to ensure both groups participate equally.

- Make sausages using playdough and practise frying them in a toy pan.

- Invite the children to blow into a paper bag and clap their hands on either side of the bag to 'pop' it. Supervise children and ensure they do not breathe in and out of the bag continuously.

What to do:

1. Invite the children to sit down and introduce the actions.

2. Start with holding up both hands with all your fingers open.

3. Make a 'pop' sound with your mouth, opening your lips quickly to let lots of air out, and make a 'bang' sound by clapping.

4. Leave a dramatic pause before the 'bang!'.

   Ten fat sausages, sizzling in the pan,
   One went pop and the other went BANG!
   Eight fat sausages, sizzling in the pan,
   One went pop and the other went BANG!

5. Continue with six, four and two sausages. Each time, hide one finger from each hand and count how many sausages remain.

Five Little Peas

Pausing before the pop!

What you need:

- No additional resources needed for this activity

Top tip

At the end of the rhyme, pause after 'the pod went...' for extra dramatic effect.

What's in it for the children?

This action song is a delight for young children; the anticipation of the loud 'Pop!' is always enticing. The song helps with the development of communication and listening skills as they await the pop. Acting out the actions and jumping to the 'Pop!' will develop gross motor skills, control, coordination and muscle strength.

Taking it forward

- Select five children to be the peas and ask them to stand in a line and 'squat' down low (on their feet not on their knees). On the 'Pop!' invite them to jump up.

- Plant some peas with the children and watch them grow.

- Practise shelling peas. This is great for improving dexterity.

- Make peas in a pod using green playdough.

What to do:

1. Sing the song slowly, showing how to 'grow' your fingers by starting with a closed fist and uncurling each finger slowly.

2. Invite the children to open their hands wider and wider to show the pea pod growing.

3. Finish with a big clap for 'Pop!'.

   Five little peas in a pea pod pressed,
   (Hold up one hand in a closed fist)
   One grew, two grew, so did all the rest.
   (Uncurl one finger at a time)
   They grew... and grew... and did not stop,
   (Open your hand wide)
   Until, one day, the pod went...
   (Open your hand even wider)
   ... Pop!
   (End with a big clap)

Popping Popcorn

Imagining cooking popcorn

What you need:

- Shakers, maracas or wave drums
- Equipment and ingredients for making popcorn (optional)

What's in it for the children?

Children are encouraged to respond to verbal cues in the song and to replicate the actions. Using percussion instruments will strengthen their hand muscles and allow them to develop musical understanding and musicality. Musical understanding is the ability to recognise rhythm in relation to creating music. Musicality is hearing and responding to rhythm using your body.

Taking it forward

- Adapt the actions to promote physical activity. Try these actions without instruments as you repeat the song:

  Popcorn kernels, (x2)
  (Slap your thighs twice, then clap twice)
  In the pot, (x2)
  (Criss-cross your hands in front of your body, like a hand jive)
  Shake them (x3)
  (Shake your whole body)
  Shake them, (x3)
  (Shake your whole body)
  Till they pop! (x2)
  (Crouch down and jump up high twice)

What to do:

1. To provide a visual representation of the song, where possible, safely demonstrate making popcorn. Ideally use a pan with a glass lid to see the transformation. Alternatively, shake popcorn kernerls in a pan or container to use as an instrument.

2. Sing the song to the tune of 'Frère Jacques'.

3. Encourage children to shake instruments to mimic the popcorn cooking and popping.

   Popcorn kernels, (x2)
   In the pot, (x2)
   Shake them (x3)
   Shake them, (x3)
   Till they pop! (x2)

Pat-a-Cake

Clapping with a partner

What you need:

- **No additional resources needed for this activity**

What's in it for the children?

Clapping along to the rhythm of the rhyme will develop children's musicality and their sense of rhythm, and can also assist with language development and learning syllables. Playing in pairs promotes social learning and cohesion.

Taking it forward

- As children become more confident with the activity, progress to different clapping routines. For example:
  - A combination of clapping hands together and clapping your hands on your thigh.
  - Clapping opposite hands. For example, children clap their right hands together, then their left hands together.
- Ask the children to create their own clapping sequences to the song.

What to do:

1. Demonstrate the actions of this song with another adult, starting slowly, clapping your hands, then your partner's hands.

2. Instead of 'mark it with B', invite the children to choose the letter of their partner's name.

3. As the children become more confident, progress to inviting them to clap their hands with a partner.

   Pat-a-cake, pat-a-cake, baker's man,

   Bake me a cake as fast as you can,

   Pat it and prick it and mark it with B (or a different letter)

   Put it in the oven for baby and me.

   For baby and me, for baby and me,

   There will be plenty for baby and me.

Five Little Men in a Flying Saucer

Getting curious about space

What you need:

- Hand puppets, stickers or props (optional)

What to do:

1. Before starting the song, hold up five fingers on one hand and count the fingers with the children.

2. Invite the children to use one hand with outstretched fingers to show the men in the flying saucer and to look around them when you sing 'left and right'.

3. They can 'Whoosh!' their arms up into the air to show the saucer flying away.

4. Hide one finger each time a man disappears.

   Five little men in a flying saucer,
   Flew around the world one day,
   They looked left and right
   But they didn't like the sight,
   So one man flew away… Whoosh!

   Four little men in a flying saucer…

   Three little men in a flying saucer…

   Two little men in a flying saucer…

5. You could add a happy ending:

   One little man in a flying saucer,
   Flew around the world one day,
   He looked left and right
   He did like the sight,
   And he decided to stay.

What's in it for the children?

This song will boost children's imaginations and curiosity about the solar system. You could ask questions like 'Where is the moon?', 'What shape is the moon?' or 'Where is the moon in the daytime?'. Dexterity is required to isolate fingers, boosting fine motor control. The song lyrics introduce children to positional vocabulary, number ordering and may also help them think about the past, present and future tenses.

Taking it forward

- You can add finger puppets or small stickers to a child's fingertips for this activity to encourage further participation.

- For older children, start the song counting down from ten, using both hands.

- Singing the song standing up will allow children to spin when they sing 'around the world' and jump or zoom around the room for 'Whoosh!'.

- Invite the children to create their own spaceship using recyclable materials.

The Grand Old Duke of York

Using positional language

What you need:

- Space to stretch and move

What to do:

1. As you sing this song, hold up both your hands to represent the ten thousand men and move them up and down as indicated in the rhyme.

2. For older children, you can invite them to sing the song while standing up and marching, crouching when you sing 'down' and stretching tall when you sing 'up'.

Oh the Grand Old Duke of York,
He had ten thousand men,
He marched them up to the top of the hill,
And he marched them down again.
And when they were up, they were up,
And when they were down, they were down,
And when they were only half way up,
They were neither up nor down.

What's in it for the children?

The song introduces lots of prepositions and positional language; using hand movements provides relevance for the language. Marching along to the song builds physical competence, postural stability, musicality and listening skills.

Taking it forward

- March around the room to the song, moving up and down as indicated.

- Clapping the song is a great way to introduce more rhythmic understanding.

- Make crowns and sing the song wearing your crowns.

- Use foil blankets and invite children to decorate them and wear them as if they were regal cloaks.

The Wheels on the Bus
Mixing movement with everyday observations

What you need:

- No additional resources needed for this activity

Top tip

Singing this song standing up offers more movement benefits, as young children will use their whole bodies to imitate the actions. For example, bouncing will extend to jumping.

What's in it for the children?

This song incorporates movement and day-to-day observations. It uses a wide range of vocabulary, including prepositions, verbs, nouns and positional language.

Taking it forward

- Allow children to add extra verses.
- Extend children's vocabulary by swapping 'the bus goes' for different nouns and verbs, for example:

The wings on the plane dip up and down...

The rudder on the boat moves side to side...

The driver in the truck bumps all around...

The wheels on the train go chug, chug, chug...

The bird in the sky soars through the air...

The bear in the woods crawls through the trees...

What to do:

1. Sing the song slowly, demonstrating each action as outlined below.

   The wheels on the bus go round and round,
   Round and round, (x2)
   (Roll your hands)
   The wheels on the bus go round and round
   All day long.

2. There are many possible variations you can try.

   The lights on the bus go flash, flash, flash...
   (Open and close your hands)

   The wipers on the bus go swish, swish, swish...
   (Swish your arms)

   The bell on the bus goes ding-a-ling-a-ling...
   (Imitate ringing a bell)

   The children on the bus bounce up and down...
   (Bounce on your bottom)

   The people on the bus go chatter, chatter, chatter...
   (Use your hands to show 'chatter')

   The babies on the bus are fast asleep...
   (Place both hands by your cheek, as if asleep)

   The mummies/daddies on the bus say shhh, shhh, shhh...
   (Place your finger on your lips)

   The horn on the bus goes beep, beep, beep...
   ('Beep' your nose)

Row, Row, Row Your Boat

Responding to music in pairs

What you need:

- Each child will need a partner

Top tip ⭐

Encourage the children to change partners. This offers the opportunity for lots of new experiences and promotes socialisation.

What to do:

1. Invite the children to sit on the floor facing a partner, with their arms outstretched and holding onto each other's hands.

2. Invite the pairs to sing the song and 'row' forward and backwards.

3. For younger children, sit them on your lap, facing you, with your hands securely placed under their arms and around their back. Slow the tempo of the song as you move.

4. There are many variations of this traditional song:

   Row, row, row your boat,
   Gently down the stream,
   If you see a crocodile,
   Don't forget to scream!
   Row, row, row your boat,
   Gently down the river,
   If you see a polar bear,
   Don't forget to shiver!
   Row, row, row your boat,
   Gently back to shore,
   If you see a lion,
   Don't forget to roar!

What's in it for the children?

When they work with partners, children develop social skills and their posture, while stimulating their sense of touch. Responding to music in pairs promotes social bonding.

Taking it forward

- Try creating your own verse which encourages a different movement. For example:

  Rock, rock, rock your boat,
  Gently to and fro,
  Wibbly, wobbly, wibbly wobbly,
  Up in the air we go!

- Try this song under a parachute, with children sitting around the edge. Rocking the parachute backwards and forwards will develop their trust in their peers and as well as their core strength.

Twinkle Twinkle Little Star

Adding a twist to a traditional song

What you need:

- No additional resources needed for this activity

Top tip

'Baa Baa Black Sheep' (page 14) and 'The Outdoors Song' (page 49) use the same tune with different lyrics. There are lots of variations to this tune, so once children know it, they can sing any number of songs!

What to do:

1. Sing the song and demonstrate the actions – slow the tempo to enable the children to do the actions.

   Twinkle twinkle little star,
   (Hold your hands up and 'twinkle' your fingers)
   How I wonder what you are!
   Up above the world so high,
   (Point up high)
   Like a diamond in the sky,
   (Make a diamond with your thumbs and index fingers)
   Twinkle twinkle little star,
   (Hold your hands up and 'twinkle' your fingers)
   How I wonder what you are!

2. Introduce a new version and imitate being in a car! There are many variations of these lyrics online.

   Twinkle twinkle chocolate bar,
   (Pretend to nibble chocolate)
   My dad drives a rusty car,
   (Pretend to drive a car)
   Turn the key and pull the choke,
   (Do a turning and pulling action)
   Off we go in a cloud of smoke!
   (Bounce up and down)

What's in it for the children?

This new version of 'Twinkle Twinkle Little Star' introduces children to varied language and can help them with their 'understanding and knowledge of the world' (as per the Early Years Foundation Stage Framework).

Taking it forward

- When you sing the chocolate bar song, you may like to alternate 'dad' with 'mum', or use a child's name.

- Suggest that the children build a car, using old cardboard boxes and loose parts.

- This rhyme evokes some lovely imagery. Encourage children to draw pictures with pencils, paints or chalk. Creating billows of swirly smoke with chalk is great for early mark making.

Frère Jacques

Introducing children to another language

What you need:

- A hand bell (optional)

Top tip ⭐

See page 17 (Crabs and Starfish), page 41 (Stars Are Twinkling) and page 30 (Popping Popcorn) for alternative rhymes to the same tune.

What to do:

1. Introduce some simple French words, such as 'bonjour' (hello) and 'merci' (thank you).

2. Showing a video of the song can help children to understand the words and story.

3. Start with an adult singing the first line and encourage the children to repeat the second line.

   Frère Jacques, (x2)
   Dormez-vous? (x2)
   Sonnez les matines, (x2)
   Ding, dang, dong. (x2)

What's in it for the children?

This song will introduce children to another language and culture. Repeating the words will develop their language acquisition, listening skills and concentration. Children will respond positively to the gentle tune and repetitive lyrics of this song. This can help them develop their awareness of rhythm.

Taking it forward

- Support cultural development by having a French day. Eat French food, listen to French music, etc.

- Once the children are familiar with the song, practise walking in a circle while singing the song: sometimes doing something physical helps make it easier to remember something.

Stars Are Twinkling

Moving in the dark

What you need:

- A dark space with plenty of room for children to move
- Torches or finger lights
- Coloured tissue paper (optional)

Top tip

Give each child a coloured piece of tissue paper and ask them to scrunch it up. Put the pieces of paper onto a parachute and make a colourful display to go with the song.

What's in it for the children?

Children will develop gross motor skills and precision movements as they practise crossing the midline axis of their bodies (this helps to develop both sides of the brain). There is a chance to learn new vocabulary too. Doing these movements in the dark allows them to have an extra sensory experience and can improve their alertness levels.

Taking it forward

- Ask the children to create their own actions to the song, boosting creative development.
- Place coloured tissue paper over the torches to make coloured light.

 Health & Safety

Remind children not to shine torches into their own or each other's eyes.

What to do:

1. Give a torch or a light to each child and ensure these are turned on before you turn off the lights.

2. Teach the actions before turning off the lights.

3. Use your own torch to model the actions while you sing the song to the tune of 'Frère Jacques'.

   Stars are twinkling,
   (Shine the lights up high)
   Way up high, (x2)
   (Wave your hands above your head)
   Bright lights shining, (x2)
   (Roll your hands)
   Catch my eye, (x2)
   (Point the lights out in front and then hide them behind your back)

Rama and Sita

Introducing Diwali

What you need:

- Torches, finger lights or glow gloves
- Dressing up items (optional)
- Materials for making lamps (optional)

Top tip

Explain that you are going to turn off the lights before you do so. Ensure that the children are familiar with the actions and can still see you to copy your movements if they need to.

What to do:

1. Introduce the Diwali story of Rama and Sita. Explain that in the story, people lit lamps to guide Rama and Sita home.

2. Give each child a torch or light. Turn off the lights once each child's torch or light is on.

3. Sing the song to the tune of 'I Hear Thunder'.

   Lights are shining, (x2)
   (Shine the lights up high)
   Follow the path, (x2)
   (Zig zag the lights)
   Rama and Sita, (x2)
   (Roll your hands up and down)
   Home at last, (x2)
   (Shine lights onto your feet)

What's in it for the children?

This song will encourage children's curiosity in different cultures. Children will gain confidence as they dance or move to the rhyme in the darkness. You can promote hemispherical development by inviting them to do movements that cross the midline axis, for example, rolling their hands to the left and the right. Hemispherical development connects both sides of the brain and involves any movement that crosses over the body, for example putting your left hand on your right knee.

Taking it forward

- Invite the children to create their own version of the song or to dress up as Rama and Sita for a role play activity.

- Add some simple Bollywood movements to the rhyme to include some complex movement patterns, especially ones that cross the midline axis.

- Make Diwali lamps (diya) using self-hardening clay, bio-glitter, paints and jewels. You may wish to add a tealight candle or a battery-powered tealight to the lamp. Be conscious of safety if you do this.

Frog Lifecycle

Talking about lifecycles

What you need:

- A visual aid to demonstrate the frog lifecycle
- Chalk (optional)

Top tip ⭐

A visual aid of a frog lifecycle could include laminated photos of frogspawn, tadpoles, froglets and frogs.

What's in it for the children?

This action song starts slowly and ends with vigorous activity. Many motor skills can be identified in this song: balance, control, coordination, strength, power, energy and stamina. The song also provides children with new vocabulary and a chance to develop curiosity about the natural world and animal lifecycles.

Taking it forward

- Research other lifecycles, for example, a butterfly, and create a similar rhyme with associated actions. Ask the children to role play becoming different creatures and see if others can identify them.

- Draw lily pads with chalk outside and encourage the children to leap from one to another. You could invite them to draw other pond creatures.

What to do:

1. I love taking this song outside. Show the children the lifecycle of a frog before introducing the song.

2. Sing the song very slowly at first as many words may be new.

3. Follow the movement suggestions as outlined and sing the song to the tune of 'Incy Wincy Spider'.

   Can you see the frogspawn, floating in the pond?
   (Squat low and bob up and down)
   Can you see the tadpoles swim merrily along?
   (Still squatting, put your hands together and swish them)
   Legs start to grow, and tail disappears,
   (Stand up)
   Froglet to frog and springtime is here.
   (Hop around like a frog)

Red Leaves Falling

Playing with leaves

What you need:

- Different-coloured fallen leaves
- A parachute (optional)
- Crayons and tracing paper (optional)

What to do:

1. Invite the children to find fallen leaves from your outside area or on a trip out.

2. Place the leaves in a heap and ask the children to select some different colours (red, gold, brown, green, yellow and orange) and then sit in a circle.

3. Sing the song standing up, dropping the leaves on the ground and picking them up at the end. The song can be sung to the tune of 'Frère Jacques'.

4. Repeat the song for different colours.

   Red leaves falling, red leaves falling,
   On the ground, on the ground,
   Autumn time is coming, autumn time is coming,
   All around, all around.

What's in it for the children?

This action song will introduce children to the beauty of nature and the changing seasons. Colour recognition is also practised during the song. I find children want to repeat this activity over and over again, which is great for physical development.

Taking it forward

- Sing the song and place the leaves on a parachute, wafting them up in the air, to represent a windy day.
- Ask the children to shake the parachute according to different weather types, for example a gentle breeze, gusty wind, or a hurricane!
- Try leaf rubbing with crayons and tracing paper to see the veins in the leaves.

How Does Your Garden Grow?

Listening to the conductor

What you need:

- Bells, castanets and triangles (or other percussion instruments)

What to do:

1. Divide the children into three groups and give the groups different instruments, for example silver bells (bells), cockle shells (castanets) and pretty maids (triangles).

2. Explain to the children that when they hear their part in the song, they must tap their instrument and then stop.

3. Adults will need to play a conductor role to encourage the children to play and stop at specific times.

4. Alternate the groups so that each child experiences the different instruments.

Mary, Mary, quite contrary,
How does your garden grow?
With silver bells and cockle shells,
And pretty maids all in a row.

What's in it for the children?

Holding and playing instruments develops children's coordination and manipulative skills, required for early mark making and writing. Tapping the rhythm of the song helps with language acquisition as children connect the syllables to the beats.

Taking it forward

- Over time, select different children to play the role of the conductor. This teaches children valuable skills: taking turns and sharing roles.

- Invite groups of three children to perform the piece to the rest of the group, standing up or sitting down.

- Research plants and flowers. Could any of them be described as silver bells, cockle shells and pretty maids all in a row?

I Hear Thunder

Adding a new verse to a traditional favourite

What you need:

- A rain stick (optional)

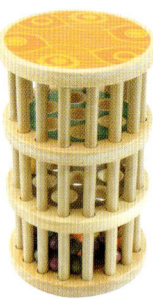

What's in it for the children?

Rain sticks are magical! Children usually watch and listen in awe and will learn to take turns while passing it around. The actions are very interactive and varied and children will enjoy the fact that the vocabulary and actions of the song are linked to daily life.

Taking it forward

- Separate the children into two groups, sitting in circles apart from each other, with an adult in each group. Sing the song as a round, with the adults leading. The second group should start singing after the first group have sung the line 'I hear thunder' twice. Singing in a round creates vocal harmonies and singing as a group develops social cohesion.

- Invite the children to draw chalk circles outside and pretend they are puddles: big, small, long and colourful. Invite the children to jump in all the puddles!

- Try making sounds using body percussion. For raindrops, use fingertips on the floor or a hard surface and for thunder, pat your thighs or stamp your feet.

What to do:

1. With the children sitting in a circle, sing the song together, passing the rain stick around the circle as you sing.

2. Add actions for the children after they have experimented with the rain stick.

   I hear thunder, (x2)
   (Hold your hand to your ear)
   Hark don't you? (x2)
   (Put your hands to your mouth, as if shouting)
   Pitter patter raindrops, (x2)
   (Wiggle your fingers from high to low)
   I'm wet through, (x2)
   (Touch your clothes)
   So are you! (x2)
   (Point to a friend)

3. Try this variation.

   I see blue skies, (x2)
   Way up high, (x2)
   Hurry up the sunshine, (x2)
   We'll soon dry. (x2)

The Outdoors Song

Moving outdoors

What you need:

- A quiet outdoor space is ideal, though this song can be sung inside with open windows.

What's in it for the children?

This activity provides an opportunity for reflection and mindfulness. Children will develop listening skills and learn to be still and notice what is around them.

Taking it forward

- Ask the children to replicate the sounds they heard, such as the sound of a car or the wind blowing.

- Embark on a nature scavenger hunt, finding natural treasures.

- Create a bird identification chart, on which children can mark off the birds they spot.

- Make some bird feeders with the children to encourage more birds into the outdoor space.

What to do:

1. Take the children outside, if possible, and introduce the song.

2. Start by singing the song with a whisper and a slow tempo to allow the children time to be still and listen. The song can be sung to the tune of 'Twinkle Twinkle Little Star'.

3. Invite the children to bring their hands to their ears, to mime listening carefully.

   Listen, listen, all around,
   Can you hear a tiny sound?
   Is the wind blowing strong?
   Can you hear the birdsong?
   Listen, listen, all around,
   What is making all the sounds?

In and Out the Dusty Bluebells

Weaving in and out

What you need:

- **Space to stretch and move**

Top tip ⭐

Be aware that initially the weaving action may be challenging for very young children as their spatial awareness and coordination are still developing.

What's in it for the children?

Standing still and holding hands requires children to have focus, attention and motor control. When they raise their hands for others to weave through, they develop the muscles in their shoulders and upper body and boost their spatial awareness.

Taking it forward

- Challenge the children's spatial awareness: rather than weaving under arms, ask them to try weaving through the other children's legs!

- Progress to a simple country dancing routine. Partner children together and encourage them to gallop up and down the room. Then ask them to make two rows with each child facing their partner, standing two metres apart. Starting at one end, the first pair of children join hands and gallop down the middle to join the opposite end. Continue until every child has had a turn.

What to do:

1. Invite the children to stand still, in a circle, holding hands with their arms raised.

2. Select one child (child 1) to come out of the circle and weave in and out under the arms of the other children. They stop behind a child (child 2) and tap them on the shoulder.

3. Repeat the song with child 2, and so on!

   In and out the dusty bluebells, (x3)
   Who will be my partner?
   Tippy tap, tippy tap, on your shoulder, (x3)
   You will be my partner.

Round and Round the Garden

Tracing body parts

What you need:

- Teddies (optional)

What to do:

1. Ask permission to tickle the child before the activity and demonstrate the actions on yourself or a teddy first.

2. Gently draw circles and 'walk', trace or gently tickle their feet or the palms of their hands.

   Round and round the garden,
   Like a teddy bear,
   One step, two steps,
   Tickle you under there!

3. Introduce a variation!

   Round and round the haystack,
   Like a little mouse,
   One step, two steps,
   Into his little house!

Top tip

Tracing fingers over the body can be very soothing prior to children's nap time, to encourage a soothing, restful sleep.

What's in it for the children?

Tactile experiences can soothe children and forge secure attachments between adults and children. Some children eagerly await the tickle, requiring timing skills and patience. The activity will build anticipation and plenty of giggles.

Taking it forward

- Invite the children to practise the actions on teddies or dolls, using 'kind, caring hands', showing positive social interaction.

- Introduce some soothing music to accompany this activity.

You Are My Sunshine

Trying sign language

What you need:

- Teddies (optional)

Top tip

Learn some simple sign language to use during the song: there are lots of videos on YouTube showing the actions using British Sign Language (BSL) or American Sign Language (ASL). The sign language actions for this song are simple and easy to follow, provided that the song is sung slowly.

What to do:

1. Sing the song slowly, pronouncing each word fully.

2. The tune is very melodic and relaxing; you may wish to sway to the melody.

3. I always finish this song with the offer of a hug!

You are my sunshine,
My only sunshine,
You make me happy,
When skies are grey,
You'll never know, dear,
How much I love you,
Please don't take my sunshine away.

What's in it for the children?

This song is very calming and can help boost children's emotional development. This song could be a good one for children to introduce to parents or carers.

Taking it forward

- Yellow is seen as a happy colour. Encourage the children to think of things which are yellow.

- Ask the children to sing and sign the song facing a friend, finishing with the offer of a hug.

- Younger children may like to rock and sing a doll or teddy to sleep with this song.

- Create a big sunshine mural on the wall and encourage children to add pictures of things which make them happy.

Humpty Dumpty

Adding a variation to a traditional song

What you need:

- Swanee or slide whistle (optional)

What to do:

1. Sit the child on your knees, holding them around the hips. Younger children should sit facing you.

2. Bounce the child to the tune. Maintaining a secure hold, lower your knees and let the child drop for 'had a great fall'. Alternatively, if you have a swanee or slide whistle, play it here to represent the fall.

3. Change the tempo of the bouncing at the end of the song.

   Humpty Dumpy sat on the wall,
   Humpty Dumpty had a great fall.
   All the king's horses and all the king's men,
   Couldn't put Humpty together again.

4. Introduce this variation with older children:

   Humpty Dumpty sat on a bin,
   Humpty Dumpty dropped and fell in,
   All the king's people looked for his head,
   But all they could find was scrambled egg!

What's in it for the children?

Humpty Dumpty was one of my children's all-time favourites. The anticipation of the 'fall' delighted them and prompted a giggle every time. This action song allows children to change the energy of their movements according to the varying tempo of the song. Involving touch stimulates the proprioceptive system, which can assist with the regulation of emotions and behaviour.

Taking it forward

- As the children become more confident with the rhyme, they may wish to use a teddy as their participant, developing leading skills, empathy and precise movements.

- Ensuring safety precautions are taken, you could demonstrate how to make scrambled egg.

Peter Hammers

Moving multiple limbs at once

What you need:

- Natural sponges (optional)

What to do:

1. With the children sitting on the floor, explain that their hands, feet and heads are going to be 'hammers'.

2. Start the song slowly and invite the children to respond by hammering with one hand (one hammer), both hands (two hammers), both hands and one foot (three hammers). Progress to using both hands and both feet (four hammers).

3. Finally, use both hands and both feet and a nodding head (five hammers)!

Peter hammers with one hammer, one hammer, one hammer,

Peter hammers with one hammer, all day long.

Peter hammers with two hammers…

Peter hammers with three hammers…

Peter hammers with four hammers…

Peter hammers with five hammers…

What's in it for the children?

This song's actions develop coordination, balance and control as children are moving multiple limbs at once.

Taking it forward

- Use natural sponges and ask the children to squeeze them with their hands and feet when hammering. This can help to improve their muscular strength and dexterity.

- If appropriate and safe to do so, introduce supervised real tool play and woodwork.

The Pirate Life

What you need:

- Pirate props (optional)

Top tip ⭐

Play the theme tune from the TV show Captain Pugwash and invite the children to make up a simple pirate dance.

What to do:

1. Provide the children with some background on a pirate's life prior to singing the song.

2. This is a long and quite complicated song, so it may take time for the children to become familiar with the words and actions.

   When I was one I sucked my thumb
   (Hold your fingers up to show the age)
   The day I went to sea,
   (Make 'waves' with one hand)
   I climbed aboard a pirate ship
   (Imitate climbing aboard)
   And the captain said to me:
   (Salute the captain)
   We're going this way, that way, forward and backwards,
   (Sway left, right, forwards and backwards)
   Over the Irish Sea,
   (Make 'waves' with one hand)
   A bottle of rum to warm my tum
   (Rub your tummy)
   And that's the life for me.
   (Swish one arm with a clenched fist)

3. Continue the song, changing some of the lyrics:

   When I was two I tied my shoe…
   When I was three I scraped my knee…
   When I was four I scrubbed the floor…
   When I was five I learned how to dive…

What's in it for the children?

Children enjoy learning about the history and the exciting lives of pirates. It also combines a range of complex movement patterns to match the language. Number sequencing is encouraged as children use their fingers to show different ages.

Taking it forward

- Introduce pirate role play and props to enhance the storytelling.

- Repeat the song standing up, encouraging full body movement.

- Create your own pirate's hornpipe dance.

A Ship Sailed from China

Swaying and using fans

What you need:

- Fans (optional)

Top tip

Try making a concertina fan by folding coloured paper. If children are having a go at this, they may require some adult assistance.

What to do:

1. Encourage the children to sway to the rhythm of the song, sitting with their legs out in front of them.

2. You could give children real or handmade fans, or invite them to make pretend fans with their fingers outstretched.

   A ship sailed from China with a cargo of tea,
   All laden with presents for you and for me.
   It brought me a fan, just imagine my bliss,
   When I found myself going…
   … Like this, like this, (x2)

3. When you repeat the song, introduce the other hand and invite children to do the fan action with both hands.

4. Then repeat the song inviting children to stay sitting with their knees bent, swaying their knees from side to side.

What's in it for the children?

This song is perfect for singing around Chinese New Year and can be a good way to introduce the children to different countries. The song also provides chances to learn new vocabulary.

Taking it forward

- Use the topic of a cargo ship to discuss where things come from. Encourage children to look at labels, for example, inside their clothes or on pieces of fruit.

Music Man

Trying instruments and body percussion

What you need:

- Percussion instruments (optional)

Top tip

Invite the children to make their own instruments using recycled and household items. They could make shakers out of bottles and seeds, guitars out of shoe boxes and rubber bands, etc.

What's in it for the children?

Inviting children to take turns to be the leader builds their confidence. Using instruments alongside the song will develop rhythmic awareness, motor skills and dexterity. Using body percussion will boost children's vestibular and proprioceptive systems through touch, movement and pressure.

Taking it forward

- Offer each child the opportunity to be the leader, building their confidence. The leader could wear a top hat!

- For older children, you may wish to create a musical ensemble with children split into groups with different instruments. Ask the children to listen and follow the conductor's lead: when their instrument is announced, they can play.

- Introduce changes of pitch, tempo and timbre. For example, asking 'How do you play?' rather than 'What can you play?' can lead to children playing slowly, quickly, loudly and quietly.

What to do:

1. For younger children introduce the song sitting down and progress to standing, then marching.

2. Once the children have adequately grasped the song and actions, lead them around the room while singing.

3. Choose a leader and ask the children to follow the 'music girl' or 'music boy' around the room, changing the 'music man' lyrics accordingly.

   I am the music man,
   I come from far away and I can play.
   What can you play?
   I play the piano!
   Pia-pia-pia-no, pia-no, pia-no. (x2)

4. Repeat the song with different instruments and body percussion:

   - *I play the cymbals…* (clap your hands)

   - *I play the drums…* (slap your legs gently)

   - *I play the triangle…* (tap your fingers)

Pass the Bag Around

Varying the pass-the-parcel game

What you need:

- A small bag containing a selection of instruments

Top tip

Keep the activity fresh by changing the instruments in the bag.

What to do:

1. Sit the children on the floor in a circle, ideally with no more than ten children per circle.

2. This game is a little like the game pass-the-parcel. Invite the children to pass the bag around the circle as you say the rhyme.

3. Whoever is holding the bag when you say 'you' may choose an instrument from the bag and play a sound.

   Pass the bag around, (x2)
   If it stops on you,
   Then you can make a sound.

4. The child puts the instrument back in the bag and the song continues until all children have been given a turn.

What's in it for the children?

Children will develop their listening, tolerance and focus skills as they await their turn to delve into the bag. Their curiosity about what's inside the bag will ensure that they remain focused and their confidence will grow as each child 'performs' their solo piece.

Taking it forward

- Place all the instruments on the floor in the middle of the circle. Have a duplicate of each instrument in a hidden spot and ask another adult to select a hidden instrument and play it (without the children seeing). Ask 'Which instrument makes that sound?'. Choose a child to play an instrument from the middle and ask, 'Does it sound the same?' Repeat with other instruments.

Coming Round the Mountain

Adding funny verses to a folk song

What you need:

- Space to stretch and move
- A tambourine or drum (optional)

Top tip ⭐

Show children videos of country line dancing and have a go at making your own line dance.

What's in it for the children?

The introduction of instruments will enhance learning opportunities for children as they listen to and respond to the rhythm. This activity offers a range of different big body movements to help children develop their locomotive control.

Taking it forward

- Invite the children to create their own verses and perhaps their own 'routines' for the chorus.
- For younger children, sit them in a circle and sing the verse together. Choose two children at a time to gallop around the outside of the circle for the chorus.
- When singing the chorus, encourage the children to gallop around the room.

What to do:

1. Introduce the song, maintaining a slow tempo with young children. Stick to two or three verses only until they remember the tune and words. You may wish to use a tambourine or drum to reinforce the rhythm.

   She'll be coming round the mountain when she comes, (x2)

   She'll be coming round the mountain, coming round the mountain,

   Coming round the mountain when she comes.

   Singing aye, aye, yippee, yippee, aye, (x2)

   Aye, aye, yippee, aye, aye, yippee,

   Aye, aye, yippee, yippee, aye.

2. Change the lyrics and invite the children to mime the different actions for each new verse.

   She'll be riding six white horses when she comes…

   She'll be wearing pink pyjamas when she comes…

   She'll be climbing up the ladder when she comes…

   She'll be driving very fast when she comes…

   She'll be rolling like a sausage when she comes…

   She'll be leaping over puddles when she comes…

   She's be wobbling like a jelly when she comes…

Miss Polly Had a Dolly

Talking about wellbeing

What you need:

- Dolls (optional)

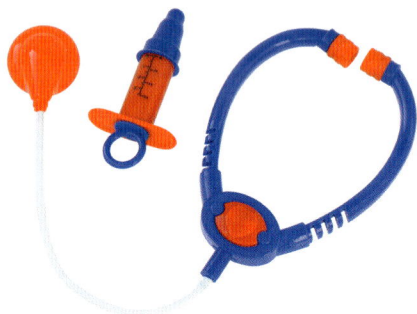

What's in it for the children?

This song provides children with an introduction to the theme of health and wellbeing. Using a doll will develop children's empathetic responses. The rhythm of the song is very memorable and the large vocabulary and repeated words boosts their language development and comprehension skills.

Taking it forward

- Ask the children to clap or play a percussion instrument every time a word is repeated, such as when you repeat 'will, will, will'. This develops their listening skills.

- Introduce some role play by asking one child to play the role of the doctor using props and another to play Miss Polly.

- Using natural outdoor resources (such as mud kitchens), invite children to create a medicine to make the dolly better!

What to do:

1. Imitate holding a baby or use a real doll for this song.

2. If you are using dolls, invite the children to sit with them in their laps as you demonstrate the actions as shown.

3. If you repeat the song, choose a different gender for the doctor, for example, swapping 'she' for 'he'.

Miss Polly had a dolly who was sick, sick, sick,
(Rock the baby)
She called for the doctor to come quick, quick, quick,
(Imitate holding a phone)
The doctor came with her bag and her hat,
(Imitate holding a bag and putting on a hat)
And knocked on the door with a rat-a-tat-tat.
(Knock on the floor)
She looked at the dolly and she shook her head,
(Shake your head)
And she said: Miss Polly, put her straight to bed!
(Waggle finger)
She wrote on a paper for a pill, pill, pill,
(Imitate writing)
I'll be back in the morning, yes I will, will, will.
(Wave goodbye)

Here We Go Round the Mulberry Bush

Getting familiar with morning routines

What you need:

- Space to stretch and move

What's in it for the children?

This song helps children to become familiar with morning routines, placing emphasis on independence and school readiness. The lyrics contain broad language content for children to practise, including familiar verbs.

Taking it forward

- Provide the children with props to support the activity, such as toothbrushes (make sure you follow health and hygiene regulations).
- Amend the song to focus on life at nursery and PSHE skills. For example:
  - This is the way we share our toys…
  - This is the way we help our friends…
  - This is the way we wash our hands…
- Invite the children to use fallen sticks and sticky tape to create their own mulberry bush.

What to do:

1. Invite the children to all hold hands and walk in a circle while singing the song.

2. Invite them to stop moving and pretend to wash their faces.

   Here we go round the mulberry bush,
   The mulberry bush, (x2)
   Here we go round the mulberry bush,
   On a cold and frosty morning.
   This is the way we wash our face,
   Wash our face, (x2)
   This is the way we wash our face,
   On a cold and frosty morning.

3. Repeat the song with different actions, encouraging the children to mime them.

   This is the way we brush our teeth…

   This is the way we comb our hair…

   This is the way we walk to school…

   This is the way we wave goodbye…

Teddy Bear, Teddy Bear

Moving the whole body

What you need:

- Teddy bears (optional)

What's in it for the children?

The movements will boost children's balance, coordination, control and posture. The song is poetic: drawing attention to the rhyming words will assist with literacy and communication skills.

Taking it forward

- Invite the children to perform this activity with real teddy bears, manipulating teddies to follow the directions of the song.

- Play the song 'Teddy Bears' Picnic' and encourage children to dance with their bears. Finish off with this teddy bear rhyme for relaxation.

- Try playing the game 'Simon says…' with teddies!

- Say the rhyme and omit some words, for example, 'Teddy bear, teddy bear, turn _____.' This will help children to develop their memory recall abilities.

What to do:

1. Ask the children to find a space on the floor. You could place sequencing markers or spots on the floor to assist them.

2. Sing the song slowly until children are familiar with the movements as outlined below.

    Teddy bear, teddy bear, turn around,
    (Slowly turn a full circle)
    Teddy bear, teddy bear, touch the ground,
    (Squat down)
    Teddy bear, teddy bear, show your shoes,
    (Raise one leg and then the other, arms outstretched)
    Teddy bear, teddy bear, that will do.
    (Put your hands on your hips and stamp your feet)
    Teddy bear, teddy bear, climb the stairs,
    (Raise alternate knees as if climbing)
    Teddy bear, teddy bear, say your prayers,
    (Imitate saying prayers)
    Teddy bear, teddy bear, turn out the light,
    (Imitate stretching up tall to click the switch)
    Teddy bear, teddy bear, say goodnight!
    (Curl up on the floor)